JANET GUTHRIE

First Woman at Indy

BY ROSS R. OLNEY

Harvey House, Publishers
New York, New York

The Author would like to thank the following for help
with this book:

Al Bloemker, Indianapolis Motor Speedway
Larry Bortstein, author
Shav Glick, Los Angeles Times
Bob Russo, Ontario Motor Speedway
Mickey Schaffer, United Press
and Janet Guthrie, herself, who contributed generously
of her time and patience on this project.

JY LV BB

Manufactured in the United States of America
ISBN 0-8178-5882-2
Harvey House, Publishers
20 Waterside Plaza
New York, New York 10010
Published in Canada by Fitzhenry & Whiteside, Ltd., Toronto

Cover photograph by Ben Ross

This book covers some of the high and low points of a long story in racing, focusing, as is only natural, on the racing driver. However, no driver ever does it alone. There are many people who contributed of their time, their talent, their spirit, and their resources along the way, and I'd like to thank just a few of them:

Ralph J. Farnham Jr. of Oceanside, N.Y., who let me work on my race cars in his shop for over ten years; Dom Galardi and Tony Buglione of A-1 Toyota, East Haven, Conn., who supported the very lean years of 1972-75; Rolla Vollstedt, who gave me the big chance to test his Championship car in 1976; Dick Simon, who had the strength of character to accept me as a teammate and whose skill in setting up chassis was so important to me at the beginning; Lynda Ferreri, whose car I drove in NASCAR for over two years; and my big-league sponsors, Bryant Heating and Cooling, Kelly Girl, and Texaco; as well as Goodyear. A special word of thanks to the United States Auto Club (USAC), the Indianapolis sanctioning organization, and to Dick King, then Director of Competition, for their scrupulous fairness and their help in the very difficult period when a woman was first breaking into oval-track racing.

—Janet Guthrie

Chapter One

None of the diners at the Victory Circle Restaurant had any idea there was a secret test out on the track that day in February, 1976. The restaurant and the Racing Hall of Fame next-door are part of the main building at Ontario Motor Speedway. Travelers on nearby San Bernardino Freeway often stop in for lunch. Huge windows in the dining area overlook the track which is located east of Los Angeles, California.

Tourists regularly see championship cars streaking by as crews tune for upcoming races. This car, a dark blue, low slung, turbocharged Indy-type car, hurtled down the long straightaway and skimmed low in the turn. Alone on the track, the echo of its thundering engine bounced off the empty grandstands.

In the pits watching was car builder Rolla Vollstedt, an expert at picking new driving talent and Dick Simon, an ace driver.

Simon, who would have a big say about whether this new driver was hired, had added some secret little tests of his own. He had changed the turbocharger adjustment slightly at each pit stop. He wanted to see if the driver had any real *seat of the pants* feel about the racer.

For this new driver could be Simon's own teammate at the Indianapolis 500 the coming May.

Finally, at one of the last pit stops before the test was over, the driver's helmet-muffled voice shouted at Simon. The words were difficult to understand over the sound of the engine, but they said "the boost seems different each time." Simon grinned, then nodded. It would be tough to find a better teammate, even if the driver was a rookie in this type of racer.

Diners in the restaurant above the track watched as the driver finally climbed from the racer. The test was over. Hands were shook all around. The deal was made.

But wait a minute! This didn't look like a stocky, hard-muscled Indy-type driver. This driver, even from far across the track, looked slim and willowy. The gestures were delicate, feminine, graceful. This was not a man, it was a *woman!*

The full face helmet came off and the auburn hair tumbled out. Sparkling eyes and a pretty face crinkled into an attractive, toothy grin of enthusiasm. Janet Guthrie, who had been adventurous all her life, had just lived through another great adventure. She was on her way to becoming the first woman ever to attempt to race at the famous Indianapolis Motor Speedway.

Not that Janet had never raced in a racing car before. Far from it! She was an experienced sports car road racer with thirteen years of driving in her past. She was good. Everyone knew that. But she was a woman. No woman had ever attempted Indy before.

Because of her experience, and of course due to the great publicity she would bring to a racing team, she had been contacted by Vollstedt the year before. He left a message on her telephone answering machine.

"Would you be interested in driving an Indianapolis car?" Vollstedt had asked.

Her reaction when she heard the tape recorded message was, "Oh, yeah...*sure!*" with an unbelieving laugh. (Guthrie's laughter is one of her most attractive features. It is deep, throaty, sincere.)

Her life in automobile racing to that point had been a struggle that had cost her most of her friends, most of her social life, and most of her time and money. Now here somebody was offering her a ride at the greatest race of all.

Besides, who in the world was Rolla Vollstedt? Janet had no idea, for she had not followed Indy-type championship racing and had never even heard of the respected auto builder.

Janet conferring with Dick Simon (left) and Rollo Vollstedt (right). (Indianapolis Speedway photos)

On the other hand, the call could have been serious. She returned the call. The test at Ontario was the result, though it took an extra year to arrange all the details.

"I was interested in Indianapolis because of Mark [Donohue] and Peter [Revson] and some other people from road racing. I had raced against them and I liked them."

But Janet Guthrie knew other women had announced to the world that they were going to race at Indy. Then they faded into obscurity. "I said yes I was interested but what I wanted was to run a test without hoopla, no big announcements about us going to Indianapolis. I just wanted to test an Indianapolis car in complete secrecy.

"If I didn't feel I could handle it, or they didn't feel I could handle it, we'd shake hands and that would be the end of it and no one would ever know."

The test was excellent and suddenly the entire racing world became aware of Janet Guthrie.

Janet posing with her racer after her successful test at Ontario.

Chapter Two

Janet Guthrie was born in Iowa City, Iowa, in 1938. Her father, an airline pilot, moved the family first to New York, then Atlanta, and finally Miami, Florida in 1941. The Guthrie family still lives on the same land in Florida. The original house, barged to the location from Key West, was eventually destroyed in a hurricane.

"My flower girl dress was lost in the storm," Janet recalls. The "flower girl" dress was used during her school years at Miss Harris's Florida School for Girls.

Janet is the oldest of the five Guthrie children. Of more than modest means, the Guthrie children attended private schools in Florida. Some of them, like Janet, graduated from these schools.

"We were comfortable," says Janet. "My family is a little eccentric and bookish. My mother always said you can do without the necessities, it's the luxuries that count.

"My dad is a very forceful individual. He is a crusader. He doesn't belong to environmental groups, but he has certainly had an impact in that area. He is not retired. My mother was going to be a doctor when she went to college, but then she married my father shortly after they graduated.

(Left) Portrait of a future Indy driver from the Guthrie scrapbook. (Top) Janet with her parents at Daytona, 1977. (Photo by Terry Adderley)

"Next to me is my brother who is a professor in Rhode Island. He was Phi Beta Kappa at the University of Iowa and has a Ph.D. from Yale University. He probably pleases my parents," she admits. Her parents have never been *that* happy with her auto racing. They do not understand Janet's desire to race though they are pleased with her success.

Next is a sister who is a librarian in Alaska, then another sister who is a potter in Boulder, Colorado, and who has great promise as an artist. Janet's apartment in New York is decorated with several fine examples of her younger sister's work. Finally comes her youngest brother who is a pilot in the mold of his father.

The Guthrie family lived far outside Miami as Janet grew up, so she turned to reading in place of playmates. She always identified with the hero, and had no trouble at all imagining going off into a jungle on safari or sailing around the Horn of Africa on a tramp steamer.

Auto Racing? "My family didn't even know about it," she says with a grin. "I hardly even knew racing existed all the way through college." She had heard of the Indianapolis Speedway, but only casually. Two of her classmates at Miss Harris's School were from Indianapolis, and often discussed the race.

"I don't know what it was about the way my parents brought us up, but I never had the feeling that I couldn't be this or that because I was a girl. I was never pressured toward the idea that the best thing was to marry and raise children . . . that there was no other option."

She was allowed to believe she could do anything.

"I was always riding off into the sunset, on some project or other."

Chapter Three

Many famous auto racing drivers grew up with the sport. They had fathers who raced, or they frequented race tracks until they became involved.

Janet Guthrie's great passion was flying.

She began to fly at the age of thirteen. "I would beg and plead to go flying so my father would teach me and I'd do things wrong and he'd yell and I'd cry, then a week later I'd be begging to go flying again," she explains in the rushed way she often speaks. At sixteen she soloed and by nineteen she had a commercial pilot's license.

Have you ever tried to talk your parents into allowing you to do something you really want to do even if it is too expensive, or too late at night, or too dangerous, or too something else? Janet Guthrie managed to talk her father into allowing her to make a parachute jump when she was sixteen. Stimulated by the books of Charles Lindbergh and her own love of flying, she agreed that her father could pilot the plane if he would allow her to jump out.

He did, and she did.

Family snapshots of Janet after her successful parachute jump, Florida, 1954. (Photos courtesy Janet Guthrie)

"I really wanted to jump out of that airplane, but I've gone on to other things. I was going with a guy much later and he decided to make a jump. I went down to the school with him but I didn't even go up in the airplane."

Racing had taken the place of flying for this girl who always wants to be on the front line — where the action is. Yet in spite of her adventurous nature, Janet Guthrie grew up to be a striking woman, slim, soft spoken, intelligent and articulate. A graduate physicist, she could choose to make a fine career in that field.

"Physics is a challenging field. I used to worry about why I liked all these men's pursuits. After a great deal of thought and reading, Freud for one, digging deep into the psychological motivations, I was forced to conclude that I did them simply because they were the most exciting and challenging things around. It was as simple as that. The fact that they were 'men's pursuits' was irrelevant."

15

Some women wave their feminism like a red flag before a herd of bulls. Some women in auto racing have done so. Not Janet Guthrie. She quietly goes about her driving and performs extremely well. She is not a feminist in the extreme sense. She believes in doing, not saying; in acting, not in parading or protesting.

Janet graduated from the University of Michigan as a physicist, working summers at an airport in Miami. One year she vacationed in Europe, hitch-hiking most of the time. "I would not have hitch-hiked in the United States but in Europe people gave you a lift for the company. I took to it with glee. They were delighted to tell you about the country you were passing through."

After she returned, she settled in Long Island and accepted a job at Republic Aviation in the aerospace division. So she needed a car to drive back and forth from work.

"What was the most beautiful car in the world? It had to be an XK-120 Jaguar," she recalls with a hearty laugh. From 1961 to 1966, while at Republic, she

(Left) Janet, in her Jaguar, competing in gymkhanas. (Right) Competing in SCCA race.

competed in gymkhanas, field trails, and hill climbs in her Jag. A naturally competitive woman, she loved the feel of the wheel and the thrill of victory. In 1962, she bought another Jaguar, an XK-140 set up for racing.

Meanwhile, in 1961 and for the first time in her life, she went to an auto race. It was at Lime Rock, a track she would race on many times in the future. She liked what she saw well enough, though she recalls there was no great burst of enthusiasm or overwhelming need to be out there on the track herself. Still, she passed the tests for a competition license from the Long Island Sports Car Club in 1962 and then the Sports Car Club of America in 1963.

As a sign of the future, she finished third in her SCCA class, far ahead of most of her classmates.

Chapter Four

Janet Guthrie had a good job. She had her club racing. She had a boy friend who cared for her and her hobby of racing. She seemed to have the best of all worlds.

In 1965 a call went out for the first women scientist-astronauts. An adventurer as always, Guthrie was one of the first to apply.

"I got through the first round of eliminations conducted by NASA. There was an exam in physics and a pilot's license requirement. I met all the qualifications except for a doctorate or experience, but I had five years in the aerospace program so I thought I'd try. At the second round of eliminations conducted by the National Academy of Sciences, I was dropped.

"I got a very nice letter from Deke Slayton saying 'nice try, but don't call us, we'll call you.'

"But by then I had become even more deeply involved in racing. Racing had pretty much taken over my life. It was becoming the next great adventure," she says with a laugh.

She was becoming an excellent mechanic as well. The 1964 Watkins Glen six-hour race, the first ever to go 500 miles, was a minor triumph for the young Guthrie. It was a National Championship race and the car, a Jaguar, had been torn down and put together bolt by bolt and piston by piston, by her. She was learning her new trade well.

Forty cars were entered in the race, with drivers like Mark Donahue and Walt Hansgen in the field. Janet Guthrie finished sixth overall, a fine finish. She was *second* in her class.

"When you start racing," she said, "you soon discover that you are not going to get very far unless you are very rich or do your own work."

Still she gave no thought to becoming a professional racing driver. She was happy with her work as a physicist and her non-professional auto racing. There was no thought of a future screaming down the straightaway at Indy or burning through the high banks of some superspeedway in a bellowing stock car. Why should there be? Why change a good life?

Eventually she did change, though, and to a life that brought her some very tough times before she became famous. When asked why, she hesitates. "The goal was never money." she explains. "The most I ever hoped for was a good ride and some sort of living. I never really expected to make any significant amount of money as a racing driver.

"I had never even seen an Indy race . . . still haven't, for that matter."

Professional racing came gradually to Janet Guthrie. It was a matter of slowly moving from one field to another, a move that even she didn't recognize at first. She did participate in some professional races like the 24 hour International Manufacturer's Championship at

Daytona in 1966, and others. Between 1964 and 1970, in fact, she successfully finished in nine consecutive runnings of the Daytona 24 hour, Sebring 12 hour, and Watkins Glen 500 endurance races. (Usually about half the field in each of these races drops out before the end.) But most of these races were for expenses, not real income. Still, she was second in class at the 1965 Watkins Glen race, second in class at the 1967 Sebring race and in 1968 she won the Governor of Florida's Award at Sebring. In 1969 she won the Falstaff Team Trophy at Sebring and in 1970 she was first in class at the Sebring 12 hours.

"Somewhere between 1966 and 1967 enough decisions were made against physics and for racing. I should have been studying for my graduate school finals and I was off racing somewhere. So I quit my job."

Janet Guthrie had become a full time professional race car driver. At 28, with several years of experience as a road racer, she was going to tackle one of the last totally male dominated fields, and for her it represented an even greater challenge.

She took all the money she had saved, sold her Jaguar to add to that, and set out to obtain for herself a ride in a race car. A ride somebody would *pay* her to take. She sent out letters and proposals and made presentations to potential sponsors and race car owners. There was plenty of racing going on, but none for a young female. Janet's fortunes began to slide. Nobody was willing to risk their race car with a woman. She had no real record on the race track, in the view of the people she was trying to reach. Everybody seemed interested in her, but nobody would say "yes."

She would stop racing team owners at race tracks and try to convince them to hire her. She would stop factory representatives and ask. She would talk to the other drivers. She was getting more and more discouraged. By the end of 1968, she was practically out of money.

She had no car of her own. She was not even club racing anymore. She took a job as a technical editor for Sperry Rand in November, 1968. She watched with some bitterness as other drivers — male drivers — started, moved up the ranks, and obtained good rides in good racing cars.

"I could have found a job in physics had I been willing to move, but I didn't want to leave New York. I was dating a guy. We had a very happy relationship for a long time, until we finally broke up." Besides, her racing operation was there. So Janet Guthrie made a very heavy decision.

(Right) Janet at Bridgehamption track, 1971. (Below) Action in the A-1 Toyota pits at Pocono International Raceway, October 29, 1972. Janet prepares to take over wheel from Dr. Arthur Mollin while Dave Schneiderman fills fuel cell. (Photo by Jeff Bienenfeld)

Chapter Five

The decision she made began the lowest period of her life. She *knew* she had to *race* for a living, no matter the cost.

"Late in 1971 I decided to start another car of my own. I would build it from scratch. I'd never built a car before but I went out and bought a brand new Toyota, drove eighty miles through a blizzard to the shop, and immediately tore it down to the last nut and bolt.

"It took all of the money I could get together. It was a major commitment. It took the whole year of 1972 to build the car, probably the worst year of my life."

Her social life stopped altogether. With some part-time volunteer helpers, she worked long nights in the garage on the car. Days she worked as a technical editor to try to support the car.

She had broken up with her boyfriend.

"It was a classic feminist bind," Janet recalls with a sad laugh. "I was unhappy, depressed, not pleased with the way my life was going and I concluded that the trouble was this guy. Then it developed that what was really wrong with my life was that I wasn't racing."

The Toyota was to be her last major effort in racing. The "2.5 Challenge Series" was a racing program for modified Datsuns and Toyotas. These exciting races were staged as companion events to the popular Trans Am series for Mustangs, Challengers and other "pony" cars of this type. Most of the big name drivers had driven in the Trans Am series: Parnelli Jones, Mark Donohue, Dan Gurney, George Follmer and Peter Revson among them. Some of them had started in the series after Guthrie, but she was a woman.

"I gave the Toyota everything I had. Days ... nights ... weekends ... all working on the Toyota. It was really very, very difficult.

"My apartment in Great Neck was nice but it went when the rent was raised. All of my money was budgeted for the race car. So I moved into a nearby room behind a store front. There were paper walls between me and the tenant who subsequently took the storefront."

Janet grimaced at the recollection. She came to dislike the tenant "up front." His business seemed peculiar, and he was often there late at night. She declared war on the man. Starting promptly at six p.m., she would try to dislodge him with Beethoven at thunderous volume.

"I tried to play fair," she recalls. "After all, he was supposed to be a business tenant."

Was it an unhappy time for the young female race car driver? "Oh yes! It was awful. It was just *awful*; it was the worst time of my life."

Janet Guthrie didn't know it then, but matters would get even *worse*. She was building the car, the 2.5 Challenge Series car, with the very last bit of her money. She was working on the car every waking moment she could spare from her job. She was alone and lonely, living in an old room with no privacy. She had only a fond hope that if she would win some 2.5 Challenge races she would attract enough attention to draw some financial support from the Toyota factory.

Finally, at long last, the car was ready. It was a little *jewel*. Janet had done a fine job on it. But before it could compete in its *first race*, the Sports Car Club of America announced that it had *cancelled* the 2.5 Challenge Series.

She had the race car ready to go, with no professional races to enter. She couldn't even drive the car to work on public streets. By then the little Toyota was a pure race car. What did she do?

"I cried a lot," she says with a wry chuckle.

A racing driver through it all, she persuaded a local Toyota dealer to pick up some of her expenses in entering the car in some amateur events. It wasn't what she wanted, but it was racing.

"I was still working as a technical editor and trying to race. I was working on the car, building the engines, towing it to the races, racing, writing and typing press releases, mailing, trying to do it all. I was worn down by the end of 1973." Still, in 1973, she was the North Atlantic Road Racing Champion. Her skills were improving all the time.

In a last desperate effort, she quit her job at Sperry, went to California and tried to persuade the Toyota factory to sponsor her. She had compiled a good record with the 2.5 Toyota in the amateur races. Leaving a lengthy and well-prepared proposal for sponsorship with the Toyota executives, she returned to the East Coast.

The garage where she worked on her car was at a boat yard, and she did odd jobs for the owner. He didn't like to drive the boat-moving truck, so Janet Guthrie drove it. For another year she worked at the boat yard and drove her Toyota in amateur races. She also wrote real estate descriptions and took any other odd job she could get.

The Toyota factory turned down her request for sponsorship. There seemed nowhere for her to go. As a pro racing driver, Janet Guthrie was failing no matter how hard she tried. In spite of the fact that she had compiled a remarkable record, she was failing.

She was flat broke, deep in debt, physically and mentally worn out, and contemplating the end of her racing career. In 1975 it seemed to her to be the end of the line.

"I was saying to myself 'Guthrie, one of these days you've got to come to your senses,'" she recalls.

Late in 1975 the Toyota factory did select her to do some public relations work, speech making and talking about small cars and safe driving in various cities. It wasn't racing, but it helped to pay for some of the bills and the rent.

Janet with her Toyota in the East Haven, Connecticut garage where she worked on the car.

Janet readying herself before a race. (Top left) Strategy session with Rolla Vollstedt and Dick Simon. (Top right) Strapping herself in behind the wheel. (Bottom left) Securing her helmet. (Bottom right) Final thoughts before taking the car out of the pits to the track. (Photo sequence by R.N. Masser, Jr.)

Chapter Six

Then, coming home one day, Janet Guthrie found the message from Rolla Vollstedt on her telephone answering machine.

Racing at Indianapolis? No woman had ever done it before. She had never *seen* an Indy car race. She certainly knew nothing about Indianapolis. It had only been a year or so that women had been allowed in the pits and garages. She knew what she would be facing if she returned the call. They would embarrass her, ridicule her, taunt her, make fun of her.

How dare she, a *woman*, attempt to invade *Indianapolis*?

The test at Ontario had to come first, and it didn't come for another year. For the Bryant Heating and Cooling Company, the sponsor, had decided to run only one car after all. That car would go to the number one driver on the team, Dick Simon. So it was 1976 before the Guthrie test at Ontario, a track almost identical to Indianapolis.

The test was not all that smooth, either. Attempting to get herself in the best possible physical shape, Janet had been doing exercises. Only two weeks before the test she broke her foot during one of her exercises. It was the first broken bone she had ever suffered in spite of her adventurous life.

"I was completely disinterested in any broken bones at that time, believe me," she explains with enthusiasm. It is not impossible to drive a championship car with a broken foot, but it is unlikely. Yet her foot was put into a cast. It was swollen, black and blue, and causing her great pain. But what about the very important test?

"I talked to a woman who was a motorcycle racer," says Janet. "All motorcycle racers are crazy. They know all about broken everything, yet she had a good head on her shoulders."

The woman friend said that postponing the test was the last thing Janet should do. Nor should she tell anybody about the broken foot. Instead, she told Janet to leave the cast on until just before the test, then to soak it off in the bathtub. Janet did, and in spite of the pain she left her crutches and walked steadily off the airplane to the terminal at Ontario. She wanted to be very steady - in case Vollstedt was watching.

She passed the Ontario test with flying colors and nobody knew until much later that her foot had been broken.

But the road to Indianapolis was still uphill. "There was an incredible amount of hostility from the drivers at the prospect of driving with any woman. I had to live with that, but it was very stressful. I had Bobby Unser, Gary Bettenhausen and Billy Vukovich all expressing themselves very clearly," she recalls with a deep, hearty chuckle. "And very *loudly*," she adds.

Just one example was what Bobby Unser said. Though he had never seen her drive, Bobby said, "I could take a hitch-hiker and teach him how to drive better than Janet Guthrie." Others said that a woman didn't have the strength or endurance to handle a race car at 200 miles per hour. The comments hurt her, Janet admits, but she forged ahead with her plans.

She needed permission from the United States Auto Club to compete in one of their races, and she needed permission from Indianapolis to drive at their track. She got the race permission and after Trenton, in which she did well until her car failed, she was accepted for Indianapolis.

Before Trenton, she was invited to a press conference. So was Indy champion Johnny Rutherford.

During a rain delay before her first Indy-type race in Trenton, New Jersey, Janet talks with former champion Jackie Stewart and sports commentator Jim McKay. (Photo by Betty Lane)

During pre-race qualifying at Trenton, Janet receives a surprise visit from A.J. Foyt. It was their first meeting. Foyt's support of Janet was important in her fight to receive proper recognition from fellow drivers. (Photo by Pat Singer)

"I had never met Johnny and didn't know much about him," said Janet, but she knew who he was. He was one of the top drivers of all. "There had been two months of this hassle and hostility and problems and nay-sayers. At the press conference I saw Johnny Rutherford on the other side of the room and I was absolutely quaking in my boots. I made myself as inconspicuous as possible.

"Then here comes this photographer. 'Hey, Johnny,' he shouted across the room, 'how about a photograph with Janet?' Oh, God," Janet thought.

Rutherford turned around, looked across the room ... and grinned broadly. He walked over and put his arm around Janet. "Why *sure!*" he said with enthusiasm.

"I just melted," said Janet.

Car problems kept her from qualifying at Indianapolis so in 1976 no woman was in the field. There was talk on the last day of qualifications that she might be offered one of A.J. Foyt's cars, but it never happened. She did practice in the car (an event that stopped much of the talk about "women drivers") and she had it up to a solid qualification speed, but she was not invited to join the team.

"A.J. said to me, 'Next time you take the car out, do this and do that and so on,' but they decided not to run a second car. I don't know why exactly."

She was disappointed, but she had come closer than any other woman to driving at Indy. Nor was she finished trying.

(Left) Janet prepares her helmet before taking out Foyt's racer during practice session before 1976 Indianapolis 500. (Right) Final words from A.J. who was impressed with Janet's skills. (Indy photos)

Janet, "in the pits," before her first stock car race at the World 600, Charlotte, North Carolina, May 1976. (Knight Publishing Co. Photo)

Chapter Seven

Instead of Indianapolis on Memorial Day of 1976, Janet Guthrie became the first woman ever to race in a NASCAR (National Association for Stock Car Auto Racing) superspeedway race. It was the World 600 at Charlotte, North Carolina. The problems started all over again with the new group of drivers.

Janet was greeted with scepticism, but she startled the "experts" by qualifying for the race and then completing the entire 600 miles without a relief driver. She finished fifteenth in her first stock car race, a fine finish. She was awarded the Curtin Turner Award for outstanding accomplishment on the race track.

But the driver problems continued. "When I was introduced to Richard Petty, I thought my fingers would get frostbitten. Ed Negre had been heard to announce that if I out-qualified him he was going to pack up and go home. I did and he was about hooted out of the race track. David Pearson, unhappily, was one of the more

Janet, being helped into the car, for the start of the World 600. (Photo by Bob Jones)

articulate spokesmen for the opposition. I'm having very little trouble now that I'm giving them a hard time on the race track," Janet says with a smile. "The situation is completely turned around from what it was at the beginning."

In that first race Richard Petty put a move on her that was unlike the NASCAR ace. "I was in turn one and I was at the bottom of the track where I should be. He opted to drop down and whiz by me about a quarter inch in between cars, probably to put the fear of God in me. It certainly didn't have any such effect," she is quick to point out.

Donnie Allison was very helpful to her from the beginning in NASCAR. And by the end of 1977, Cale Yarborough, the reigning NASCAR champion (and a former critic) was heard to say, "There is no question about her ability to race with us. More power to her. She has 'made it' in what I think is the most competitive racing circuit in the world."

Janet was also racing in Indy-type Championship races, breaking the existing women's world closed course speed record when she qualified twelfth for the Indy-car race at Michigan International Speedway with a run of 186.48 miles per hour. In several NASCAR races, in 1976 and 1977, she out-qualified Johnny Rutherford. During one race she screamed past none other than David Pearson. Finally her engine blew, but until then she was racing up front.

Even though it was her rookie (first) year in NASCAR and she was working with a brand new crew and an unfamiliar car, she was having a fine year. She had ten finishes in the top twelve that first year.

In the final NASCAR stock car race of the year at Ontario Motor Speedway, she led at one point. *Stock Car Magazine* said,"One of the best races of the afternoon was between Bobby Allison and Janet Guthrie. They swapped positions back and forth and ran side by side trying to outbrave each other in action that had the veterans shaking their heads. It was some fine show." Janet's car failed only twenty-four laps from the end.

But it was in May, 1977, that Janet Guthrie made the most history. She qualified, and then raced, in the Indianapolis Speedway Race. When her white and green Number 27 thundered into the first turn lap, the biggest barrier fell. Something that had never been done before, something that was never expected to be done, happened. A woman was in the field for the Indy 500. Her car suffered mechanical problems and she eventually dropped from the race, but while she was on the track she drove very well.

"When the green flag comes down there is room for only one thing in your mind. That is strict attention to what's going on in the race and how best to do what you want to do there. As far back as I was in the field (she still out-qualified almost half the field, including several experienced Indy drivers) I had planned only one thing and that was if anything happened in front of me I wanted the time and distance to stay out of it. This meant keeping my position reasonably well, standing on the gas, but mainly making sure my position was right with the other cars. You can't start like a real mouse or you will get run over from behind. My main objective on the first lap was completing the first lap."

Janet Guthrie is a pretty woman with a well-modulated voice that has only a trace of the "interview twang" apparent on race track Public Address systems. She has a curious way of ending many words with an upbeat, not at all unattractive. She seems casual, friendly and open. She is a resident of Florida but spends much

(Top) Janet, at the 1977 Indianapolis 500, leaves pits to reenter race. (Photo by Ross R. Olney) (Below) The end of the race for Janet. She impatiently waits while her crew tries unsuccessfully to repair her racer. (Photo by Marty)

of her time in her East Side New York City apartment. The apartment is large enough to be comfortable without being at all lavish. It has books, potted plants, stereo equipment; but still it seems somewhat sparse. It seems to belong to a traveling person, as indeed it does.

There is one other obvious difference between this apartment and the hundreds of others in the same building.

Over the kitchen stove where normally might be pots and pans or some colorful tile there is a huge photograph. It fills the wall and dominates the kitchen. It depicts the apartment owner sitting on the roll bar of a sleek racing car at Ontario Motor Speedway. Her smile of triumph includes no indication of her painfully broken foot. The photo was shot on the day of her test.

So the battle was over and because of Janet Guthrie women had become an accepted part of big time auto racing? The fight had been won?

No!

Sponsorship money was still hard to find. Janet continued to race on the NASCAR trail and qualified for both the Pocono 500 and the California 500 in 1977, but car problems forced her out. She raced in nineteen NASCAR races and was high on the list for "Rookie of the Year" honors. Her Kelly Girl Chevrolet became a familiar sight battling fender to fender with the cars of the "good ol' boys."

At Talledaga, Janet's Kelly Girl stock car, #68, lines up ahead of Richard Petty's famous #43. Janet had the last laugh on Petty, one of her harshest critics, by outqualifying him for the race. (Photo by Dorsey Patrick)

In Vollstedt's cars, she had entered eleven races and only finished two, neither without problems. She had proven that a woman could qualify and drive in the Indianapolis Speedway Race, but could a woman ever finish the grueling 500 miles? Most said, "No."

"Can you physically compete with men?" people would ask her point-blank. Guthrie would just smile. She'd heard it before.

She would politely answer the question over and over again. "I *drive* the car, I don't carry it."

After the 1977 Indy race, Janet Guthrie was confident. She had barely missed qualifying in one Indy race and had raced in the next. She had been the fastest qualifier during that second weekend of time trials. She had qualified faster than nearly half the field. Any rookie who had done that well could reasonably expect to be offered a ride for the next race — probably in a better car and probably quickly, before some other car owner offered.

Janet sat on pins and needles and waited. The call

didn't come in June or July or August. Other rookies were racing on the Championship Trail, building a name for themselves. In September she started placing calls herself. Still no offer of a car came.

It seemed impossible to imagine that the first woman driver at Indy was going to go without a car for the next Indy race. Christmas and New Years' passed. Other rookies had their assignments and were awaiting tire testing programs (and car testing) the moment the snow melted in Indiana. Still Janet Guthrie had no car.

Meanwhile, another blow hit her. She learned that Kelly Girl, her NASCAR stock car sponsor, was going to cut back their program severely. She had no championship car ride. She was one of the most famous women in racing, but she was also nearly out of racing. Janet was bewildered and frustrated.

She didn't quit, though. Tired and disappointed, she started the rounds all over again. She started to knock on doors, to try to interest anybody in sponsoring her at Indy.

The doors were closed. "I represented half the human race and it still wasn't enough to get a champ car sponsor," she lamented. Her friends couldn't help, her agent couldn't help, and her excellent racing background wasn't helping either.

Time was running out.

(Above) Janet with her NASCAR stock car. (Below)Janet, #68, battling Bobby Allison, #12, in NASCAR action. (Photo by R.N. Masser, Jr.)

Janet, hot, sweaty, and exhausted, after six-hour endurance race at Watkins Glen, July 1977. (Photo by Joseph P. Lippincott)

Chapter Eight

Making an appearance on television on the last day of March, 1978 (for she was still a famous figure), Guthrie said, "It looks like I'm not going to be at Indianapolis this year."

She was wrong. Texaco was watching. Later that same day, Guthrie had her sponsor. She would need one month to prepare a car before the track opened at Indianapolis. She had her month, but just *barely*.

What a sponsor she found! The Texaco company gave her the budget she needed — more than $100,000 to buy a car, hire a crew, and then get the car in the field in the 1978 race. She was in complete charge. She could do whatever she felt was right, buy the car she felt was best, hire a crew in whom she had confidence. She could succeed or fail, but the credit, or the blame, would be hers alone.

It wasn't the three million invested by teams like Roger Penske's, but it was a *ride* at *Indy*. It was more than some of the other drivers had. It was enough money to get a car and a crew.

Laughing and happy once again she said, "What a difference a week makes!" for still another sponsor had turned up at the last minute. Guthrie hired Kenny Ozawa as her chief mechanic. She quickly sent her entry blank to Indy officials. Her name appeared on the list. She had made it.

Meanwhile, she bought a racer. For 1978, with Texaco's solid backing, Guthrie obtained a George Bignotti-built Wildcat. It was a solid, competitive racer. The car was painted a bright red and white, a pink stripe was added around the cockpit, and the car was then named *Texaco Star*. It looked *fast*.

It *was* fast. On the second weekend of qualification runs (the first weekend was rained out), Janet was ready. With many on the sidelines hoping she would fail, she streaked the new car around the Speedway at an average speed of 190.325 miles-per-hour. Her position in the starting field was on the outside of the fifth row, a *fine* starting spot. Because she was ready on the first day, and fast, she was starting ahead of drivers like Bobby Unser, A.J. Foyt, Gary Bettenhausen and Jim McElreath. She was starting the Indy 500 ahead of eighteen of the best drivers in the world.

Race day dawned hot, muggy and clear. From all around, long lines of cars and buses snaked toward the Speedway. Soon nearly 400,000 people jammed the long grandstands and vast infield of the old 2½ mile track. It was more people than had ever gathered at one time for a sporting event anywhere in the world, anytime in history. Many of the racing fans had come to see if a woman driver, Janet Guthrie, could last in the big race with a good car. Last year hadn't really been a fair test. But this year her car was reliable, her starting position excellent. This year would tell a story where female drivers were concerned.

A happy Janet, trying out her new Texaco Star racer before the 1978 Indianapolis 500. (Texaco photo)

Janet steers the Texaco Star onto the track at Indy for practice session before race. (Indianapolis Speedway photo)

The parade lap, the pace lap, and the thirty-three fast cars thundered into the first turn. The race was on! Guthrie, in mid-pack, appeared smooth and in complete control.

She had said before the race that she was going to stick to her planned strategy no matter what happened. She wasn't going to charge for the lead at the beginning against drivers like Tom Sneva, Al Unser, Danny Ongais and Johnny Rutherford. That would be foolish, she knew. Her four-cylinder engine was no match for the V-8's of the leaders, but she hoped the V-8's would not be as reliable. She planned to drive her own race. She would set a pace and stay with it; conservative at first, strong at the end. She would allow the other drivers to battle it out and ruin their cars. There's an old maxim in racing that says, "In order to win, you have to finish," and she wanted to be there when the checkered flag was waved. If she could finish, and if the V-8's didn't, she hoped she could place among the top five.

There is a tall, four-sided, five foot square tower near the start-finish line at Indy. On it, from top to bottom, in electric light numbers, are the positions of all thirty-three cars in the race. At the top is the number of the leader, then down to the last place car at the bottom of the tower. The numbers constantly move about as positions in the race change. The tower is visible to hundreds of thousands of fans along the main stretch.

Car Number 51, the Texaco Star, was two-thirds of the way down, but steady. On the track, Janet Guthrie was driving her own race. If a much faster car drew up behind her, she would carefully move over and allow him to pass (which is standard track etiquette). She knew that many of the front runners would have problems and drop out. She knew that many of the tail enders just couldn't match her own speed. She wanted desperately to finish the grueling race.

Gradually, almost without the fans noticing it, the Number 51 began to move up the tower. Before, it had been down around eighteenth place, now it was moving up to seventeenth, then sixteenth, then fifteenth. Guthrie was bettering her position so smoothly that nobody was noticing. Her strategy was working. Even the frantic radio and television announcers failed to relay the gradual move forward.

The numbers shifted again and car 51 was in fourteenth place. Then thirteenth. Guthrie's pit stops were smooth and without serious problems. The bright red and white car with the star would glide in, take on fuel, and streak back into the race almost before anybody but the crew noticed. The tower went to twelfth place. Not only was Guthrie remaining in the race, she was at the halfway point leading many famous drivers. Up front, Danny Ongais was battling with Tom Sneva and Al Unser. Others had dropped out with car problems. Guthrie's pre-race strategy seemed to be paying off.

Of course, running in twelfth place in the Indy 500 and finishing in twelfth place were two different matters. The race would grind on and eventually the black-markers would turn up their boost and make a hard drive for the money.

Guthrie sped on, her car almost as though it were on a rail. She didn't waver as she guided the Texaco Star down the straightaways and around the four corners. Suddenly the numbers on the tower changed again. Janet Guthrie was in eleventh place. She had moved up again. It suddenly appeared possible that she could not only finish the race, but that she could race for awhile in the top ten. No woman had ever done that in USAC either. Or, with luck, even *finish* in the top ten. That feat had not been considered possible in view of the intense competition and superb racing cars in the race.

Near the end, as more and more cars dropped out with mechanical problems while Guthrie maintained her pace, the number changed again. Car Number 51 had moved into tenth place. She was in the top ten. She knew it, there in her speeding car. It was hot, she was cramped, she could hear noises in the car she didn't like, but she was very happy. So far, so good.

Tenth place. If only she could *finish* there, it ought to establish the capability of women in racing. She would be a regular, every-day, competitive, championship race car driver. Nothing more, nothing less. That was all she asked before the race started.

Down the straightaway during the 1978 Indianapolis 500. The racer performed up to all of Janet's expectations. (Speedway photo)

Besides, she could hope that Texaco would continue to sponsor her in other races if she could finish in the top ten. They had already received millions of words of favorable publicity for their sponsorship. They were certain to get more if she could maintain her pace and the Texaco Star could hold together.

She did, and it did. Before the 1978 race ended, the numbers shifted again. In a fine, consistent drive for the finish, after turning up the boost at the halfway point, Janet Guthrie moved up one more place. She finished in ninth place, solidly in the top ten, to win nearly $25,000.

Grinning broadly, she greeted the crowd of newsmen and women as they pressed around after the race. More had followed her than had followed the winner of the race, Al Unser. She brushed her hand through her hair, grinned, and hugged her crewmen. She didn't look as though she had just driven an intensely competitive 500 mile race. She was cool, clean, calm and collected, and very, very happy. Finally she spoke.

"I hope this ends the nonsense once and for all that a woman can't compete in these cars. Nobody would pay any attention to the fact that I had been running 500 miles in stock cars, a much tougher job than this physically — although these cars demand total precision, which is mentally grueling. '

"Just remember, too, that the driver is the most visible part of the team. But the crew is most important. I had, I believe, the best crew in Gasoline Alley."

Janet in a pensive yet content pose among all the excitement of the Indianoplis 500. (Speedway photo)

As the crowd of reporters and fans cheered, others along pit row began to realize what had happened. A woman had finished the Indy 500 for the first time. Further, she had finished in the top ten, where only USAC stars usually reside. Guthrie, they realized, had become a USAC star.

Only two things remain for her to do at Indy.

One, to win the 500.

And two, to finally get somebody to install women's facilities in the garage area. Janet is the first to point out that other young women drivers are battling their way up. They will eventually knock on the Indianapolis door.

ABOUT THE AUTHOR

ROSS R. OLNEY has written more than eighty books for children, young adults and adults; many in the fields of sports and the outdoors. He lives in Ventura, California with his wife and two of his three sons. Another Harvey House favorite by Mr. Olney is *Illustrated Auto Racing Dictionary For Young People.*